BIRMINGHAM CITY UNIVERSITY
Book

KU-567-557

BIRMINGHAM CITY
LIBRARY
UNIVERSITY

Curriculum Visions

The Weather Book

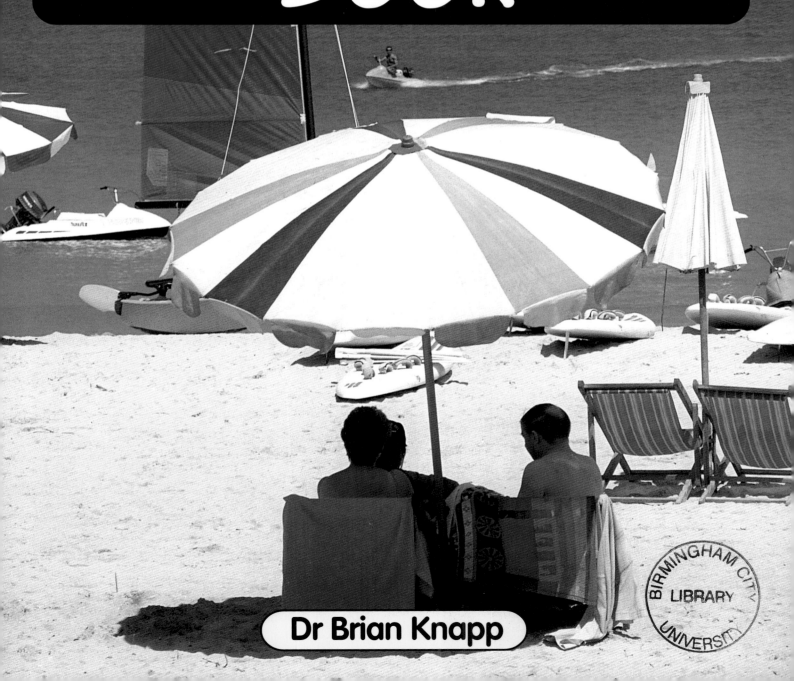

Dr Brian Knapp

✦ Atlantic Europe Publishing

First published in 1998 by
Atlantic Europe Publishing Company Ltd

Copyright © 1998
Atlantic Europe Publishing Company Ltd

All rights reserved. No part of this publication
may be reproduced, stored in a retrieval
system, or transmitted in any form or by any
means, electronic, mechanical, photocopying,
recording or otherwise, without prior
permission of the Publisher.

Author
Brian Knapp, BSc, PhD
Art Director
Duncan McCrae, BSc
Editors
Elizabeth Walker, BA and Mary Sanders, BSc
Illustrations
Digital illustrations by David Woodroffe
Cover illustration by Simon Tegg
Designed and produced by
EARTHSCAPE EDITIONS
Reproduced in Malaysia by
Global Colour
Printed and bound in Italy by
L.E.G.O. SpA
Suggested cataloguing location
Knapp, Brian
　　The Weather Book
　　1. Weather – Juvenile Literature
　　I. Title. (Series: *Curriculum visions*)
551.6

ISBN 1 862140 71 5 Hardback
ISBN 1 862140 76 6 Paperback

Picture credits
All photographs are from the Earthscape
Editions photolibrary except the following:
(c=centre t=top b=bottom l=left r=right)
Courtesy of the University of Dundee 30br;
NASA 40tr, 43br; NOAA 39tl, 41cr; ZEFA 21cr,
25t, 39tr.

*This product is manufactured
from sustainable managed
forests. For every tree cut down
at least one more is planted.*

Mountain cloud

Curriculum Visions

Glossary
There is a glossary on page 46. Glossary
terms are referred to in the text by using
CAPITALS like this.

Index
There is an index on page 48.

There's more on the Web
This is a web-linked book. You will find
more free information, photographs and
detail about topics in this book by visiting
our world wide web site:

www.CurriculumVisions.com

Winter snow

There is a **teacher's guide**, **weather adventure stories** and
other support material to accompany this book. These are
available only directly from the publisher.

Contents

BIRMINGHAM CITY ⋯⋯VERSITY
Book no. 34534881
⋯ject no. 551·6 Kna
LIBRARY

Winter sunset

Weather

These are some of the ways WEATHER affects us.

1. We feel weather through **SUNSHINE**, **HEAT**, **RAIN** and **WIND**. Find out about the instruments that measure these things on pages 7, 14 and 18.

2. Temperatures change throughout the day. Find out what pattern the changes make on page 9.

3. When **MOISTURE** in the air turns to droplets of water, it makes **CLOUDS**. Clouds, rain and snow are explained on pages 12, 20 to 27.

4. The weather changes throughout the year, giving us our **SEASONS**. See two kinds of seasons on pages 10 and 16.

5. When air moves quickly, we feel it as wind. The fastest winds are **GALES**, **HURRICANES**, **CYCLONES**, **TYPHOONS** and **TORNADOES**. These are explained on pages 18, 38 and 40.

6. Air picks up moisture from the sea and from plants. Find out about the results of **EVAPORATION** on page 12.

7. If air cools near the ground, **CONDENSATION** occurs and we get **DEW** or **FOG**; if it is very cold, we get **FROST**. See how this happens on pages 12 and 13.

8. The air takes its warmth from the land or sea. Find out what happens to air that is warmed and air that is cooled on pages 8, 21, 32 and 34.

9. See how **CUMULUS**, **CIRRUS** and **STRATUS** clouds form on pages 20 to 23 and 26.

10. Thick, dark clouds usually produce rain. Find out about how rain forms on page 12.

11. Towering clouds bring **THUNDER** and **LIGHTNING**. Find out about thunder and lightning on page 24.

12. Where air sinks, clouds often disappear. Find out about **RAINSHADOWS** on page 27 and **HIGH PRESSURES** on page 28.

13. Where air rises, changeable weather usually occurs. Find out about **LOW PRESSURES** on page 30.

14. Hills, valleys and coasts cause their own **LOCAL WEATHER**. Find out about this on pages 32 and 34.

15. People who live in cities have warmer weather than those in the neighbouring countryside. Find out about **CITY WEATHER** on page 36.

16. The weather near the Equator is very different from the weather near the poles. Find out about **CLIMATES** on page 42.

17. Changes in one part of the world can affect the climates worldwide. See how **GLOBAL WARMING** and **EL NIÑO** work on page 44.

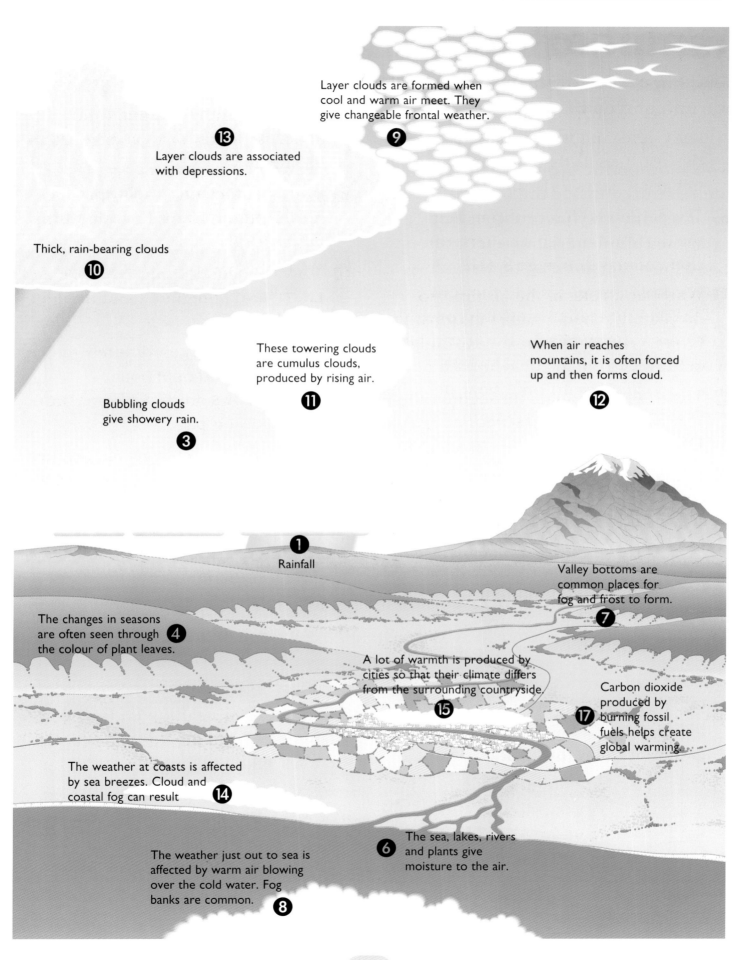

Layer clouds are formed when cool and warm air meet. They give changeable frontal weather. **9**

Layer clouds are associated with depressions. **13**

Thick, rain-bearing clouds **10**

These towering clouds are cumulus clouds, produced by rising air. **11**

When air reaches mountains, it is often forced up and then forms cloud. **12**

Bubbling clouds give showery rain. **3**

1 Rainfall

Valley bottoms are common places for fog and frost to form. **7**

The changes in seasons are often seen through **4** the colour of plant leaves.

A lot of warmth is produced by cities so that their climate differs from the surrounding countryside. **15**

Carbon dioxide produced by **17** burning fossil fuels helps create global warming.

The weather at coasts is affected by sea breezes. Cloud and coastal fog can result **14**

The sea, lakes, rivers **6** and plants give moisture to the air.

The weather just out to sea is affected by warm air blowing over the cold water. Fog banks are common. **8**

Temperature

One important way that we notice the weather is through temperature – warmth and cold.

Imagine spending a night in a tent with snow on the ground! The temperature outside the tent can be unpleasantly low (picture ①). But even the thin material of a tent offers enough shelter for it to be warmer – even comfortable – inside the tent.

You might think you would prefer to be on a sunny beach. But it can be scorching hot on the beach, and much more pleasant on a boat or under the shade of a beach umbrella (picture ②).

In each of these cases we notice the heat and cold as pleasant or unpleasant, and we also notice that there are ways we can make improvements to make ourselves

more comfortable (picture ③). And this is very much how we see the weather – something to be enjoyed or something we have to cope with.

▲ ② The air is cooler in the bay because it is sharing its heat with the cool water.

▼ ① The air is warmer in the tent because it is trapped inside.

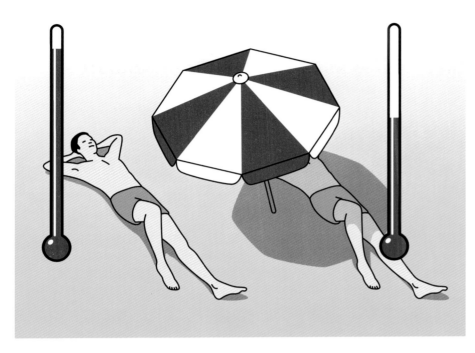

▲ ③ **Sun and shade**
If you place a thermometer in direct sunlight, the liquid in the tube rises. This is because the liquid is absorbing heat from the sun and expanding. Take the thermometer into the shade and the liquid in the tube falls to show the air temperature.

Thermometers should always be placed in the shade so that they record the warmth of the air, not the direct heat of the sun.

Measuring heat and cold

To make sense of the weather, we need to measure things like temperature accurately. Temperature is measured using a **THERMOMETER**.

Simple thermometers are glass tubes partly filled with a coloured liquid (picture ④). The change in length of the liquid is measured using a scale.

▶ ④ Liquids expand when they get warmer, and contract when they get colder. So the height of the liquid in the tube tells us how warm the air is. In a thermometer the liquid is trapped in a very narrow tube and this makes even small changes easy to see.

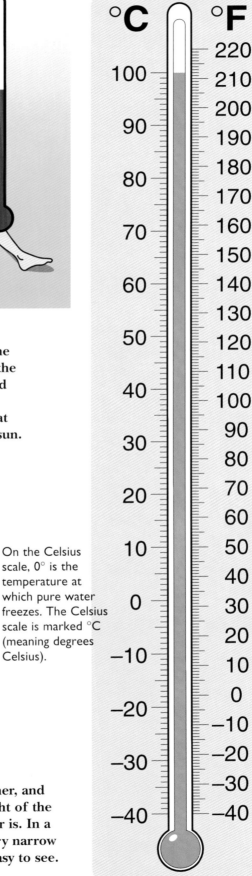

On the Celsius scale, 0° is the temperature at which pure water freezes. The Celsius scale is marked °C (meaning degrees Celsius).

On the Fahrenheit scale, the freezing point of water is 32°. This scale is marked °F (meaning degrees Fahrenheit).

Daily temperature changes

Changes in temperature through the day occur because of warmth from the Sun during the day and cooling down during the night.

Have you noticed that the warmest part of the day is in the early afternoon, not at midday when the Sun is highest? This is because, when the Sun shines, it does not warm the air directly, but first warms the ground (or the sea) which, in turn shares its warmth with the air (picture ①).

Because it takes time for the ground to share its heat with the air, there is a delay between the time when the Sun is highest in the sky and the time when the air is warmest.

During the night, the ground and the air lose heat to space, and so cool down. This is the daily pattern everywhere in the world. Wherever you are, it is coolest just after dawn and hottest in the early afternoon.

Plotting daily temperature

If you were to measure the temperature throughout the day, you could plot the results as a graph like the one on the opposite page (picture ②).

The two temperatures that most easily sum up the whole day are the hottest (**MAXIMUM**) and coldest (**MINIMUM**). These are the figures given by most weather forecasters.

An easy way to measure the maximum and minimum temperatures in a day is to use a special maximum–minimum thermometer (picture ③).

▶ ① The way the air is heated

1. The heat from the Sun passes through the air and heats the ground.

2. Then, the heated ground shares its heat with the air.

Sun

◀ At dawn each day the Sun rises. It is at its highest at noon. It then sinks again, disappearing at sunset. This pattern is shown here.

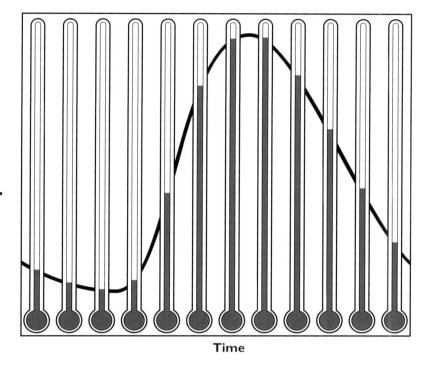

Temperature

Time

◀▼ ② How to make a graph of temperature changes throughout the day

◀ If we sketched a thermometer every two hours during the day and then placed the sketches side by side, we would get this picture. It shows directly how temperature changes.

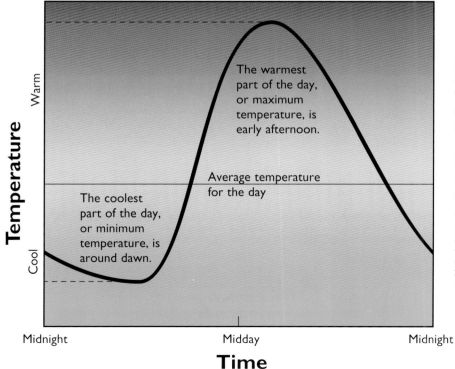

Temperature

Warm

Cool

The warmest part of the day, or maximum temperature, is early afternoon.

Average temperature for the day

The coolest part of the day, or minimum temperature, is around dawn.

Midnight   Midday   Midnight

Time

◀ This graph shows the temperature changes during a day.

▶ ③ This maximum–minimum thermometer will tell you the highest and lowest temperatures of the day.
  The tube contains two small metal markers that are pushed by the mercury as it moves around the U-shaped tube. The markers are held in their farthest positions by a magnet behind the scale.

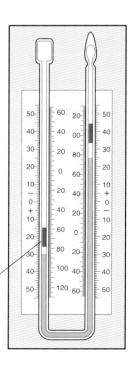

Metal marker

Seasonal temperature changes

Temperatures in some parts of the world change with the seasons. But this is not true everywhere.

You *can* tell the SEASONS by looking at the way plants behave (picture ①). But if you made a graph of the average temperature for each month, you would be able to see the way changes occur much more accurately.

Plotting the seasons

The graph opposite shows the pattern throughout the year at Oxford, England (picture ②). Oxford is about half-way between the Equator and the poles. This kind of location is often called the **MID-LATITUDES**.

Notice how it is coldest in January and February and warmest in July and August. This gives the temperature seasons – Spring, Summer, Autumn and Winter.

The seasons lag behind the sun

On page 8 we saw that the hottest time of day was later than when the Sun was highest in the sky. The same delay also happens in a year. The Sun is highest in the sky at the end of June, but the hottest time of the year is a month later.

The Sun is lowest in the sky, and shines for the shortest time, in December, yet the coldest time of the year is in January and February.

This is because it takes time for the ground to warm up each Spring. It also takes time for the ground to cool down each Autumn.

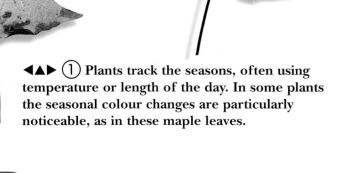

Late Autumn

Early Autumn

Late Summer

◀▲▶ ① Plants track the seasons, often using temperature or length of the day. In some plants the seasonal colour changes are particularly noticeable, as in these maple leaves.

▼ ② This is a yearly temperature chart for Oxford, England. The top part of the chart shows the Sun at noon. The lower part shows the average temperature for each month.

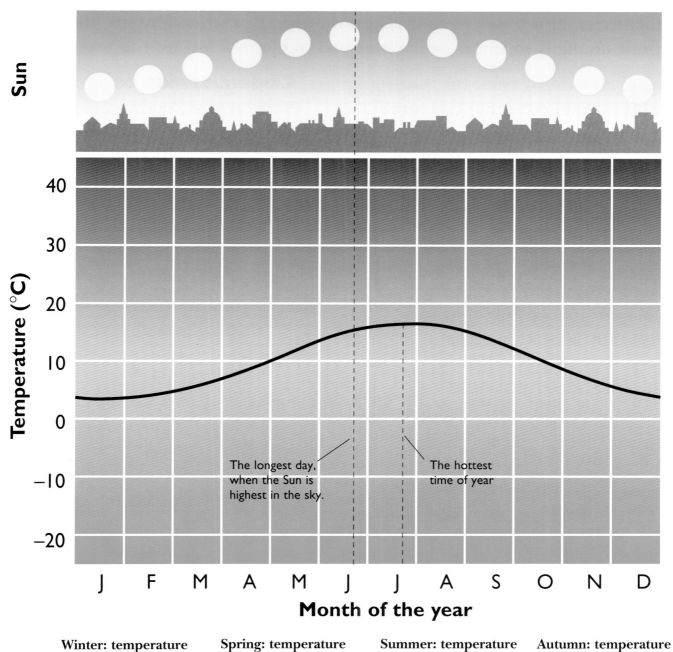

Sun

Temperature (°C)

The longest day, when the Sun is highest in the sky.

The hottest time of year

J F M A M J J A S O N D

Month of the year

Winter: temperature at its minimum

Spring: temperature rising

Summer: temperature at maximum

Autumn: temperature falling

Rain, snow, dew and frost

Moisture is all around us as invisible vapour. But when air gets cold, the vapour changes to water or ice, not just in clouds, but on the ground as well.

We are all used to **RAIN**, but water in the air occurs in three forms: moisture (vapour), liquid (cloud droplets and rain) and solid (ice crystals in the shape of **SNOWFLAKES**) (picture ①).

Condensation

When water changes from liquid to invisible moisture, we call it **EVAPORATION**. When it changes back from vapour to liquid, we call it **CONDENSATION**.

Cloud and rain

Strangely, it is easy for water to evaporate, and much more difficult for it to condense. Condensation needs a surface for the vapour to condense on to.

Specks of dust occur by the million in the air. When moisture

▼ ① **This diagram shows the many ways that condensation can occur. The movement of water from clouds to air, to ground, to clouds, is called the WATER CYCLE.**

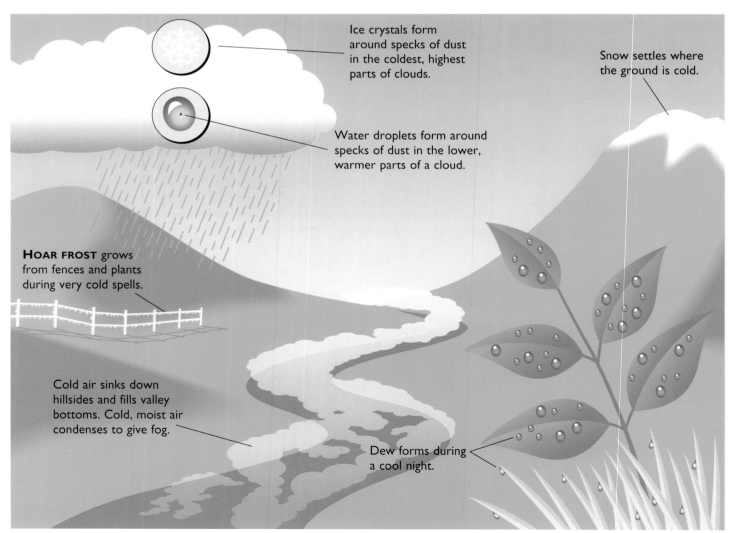

Ice crystals form around specks of dust in the coldest, highest parts of clouds.

Snow settles where the ground is cold.

Water droplets form around specks of dust in the lower, warmer parts of a cloud.

HOAR FROST grows from fences and plants during very cold spells.

Cold air sinks down hillsides and fills valley bottoms. Cold, moist air condenses to give fog.

Dew forms during a cool night.

▶ ② The amount of rain that falls depends on how much moisture is in the air. On hot days, large amounts of moisture are in the air, and when the moisture turns to droplets, torrential rain can be produced.

condenses on them, they make tiny beads of water called droplets. We see these as a **CLOUD**. When they fall from the cloud, rain occurs. We call the rain **DRIZZLE** if the drops are small (picture ②).

Dew and frost

When moisture condenses on the ground, we call it **DEW**. If the moisture then freezes, we call it **FROST** (picture ③).

▲ ③ When the air is very cold, vapour changes to ice and builds up as frost. You can see the individual ice crystals on this plant.

Snow

Ice crystals form in cold clouds around specks of dust. Snowflakes are made of many tiny ice crystals clumped together. A combination of snow and wind produces a **BLIZZARD**.

Mist and fog

Cloud close to the ground gives **MIST** or **FOG**.

Mist and fog are described in terms of how far you can see, or visibility.

Mist is when the air is not clear, but when you can see at least 1 km.

Fog is when the distance you can see is less than 1 km. Dense fog normally refers to a visibility of less than 100 m.

By the way... The general name for all kinds of liquid and solid forms of water is PRECIPITATION.

Measuring and charting rainfall

Rain gives the moisture that allows plants to grow. Too much rain makes flooding likely; too little rain gives droughts. Measuring rain tells us what to expect.

We might think that cold days are unpleasant, but days without rain can spell disaster for crops and our food. This is why it is important to know how much rainfall to expect and how variable it is likely to be.

Rain is measured using a **RAINGAUGE** (picture ①). A raingauge is easy to make, but placing it incorrectly can lead to errors.

Measuring rain

Rainfall is most commonly measured in millimetres. This small unit is used because, in most places, only small amounts of rain fall each day.

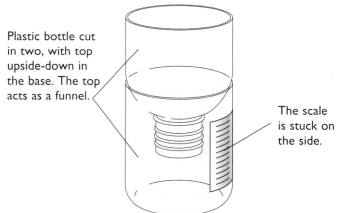

Plastic bottle cut in two, with top upside-down in the base. The top acts as a funnel.

The scale is stuck on the side.

▲ ① To make a simple raingauge, cut off the bottom of a soft-drinks bottle. Turn the top upside-down and use it as a funnel. Place the raingauge inside a flower pot large enough to leave a wide gap all around the raingauge. Bury the flower pot in the ground so that the rim of the raingauge is level with the ground.

To make a scale, pour known amounts of water into the raingauge from a scientific measuring jar and mark the different levels on the side of the gauge.

Where to place the gauge

Watch rain falling on a windy day and you will start to see why it is important to place a raingauge carefully if you are to collect a fair sample (picture ②). The wind can

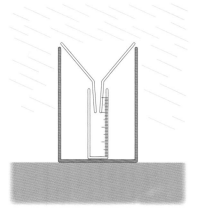

▲② This raingauge is standing up in the wind. The rain falls at a slanting angle and the raingauge does not collect it all. This is the reason why many raingauges are placed level with the ground.

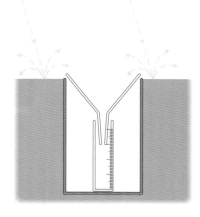

▲ ③ This raingauge has been placed level with hard ground. When heavy rain falls, some of the rain splashes off the hard ground and into the gauge, and too much rain is collected. This is the reason why many raingauges are placed in grassy fields. The upright blades of grass prevent rain splashing about.

swirl air around a raingauge which is standing high above the ground. To avoid errors caused by strong wind, it helps to place the rim of a raingauge level with the ground.

To stop water splashing into the raingauge from the surroundings, it is best to place a raingauge on a lawn or on gravel (picture ③).

Making a rainfall chart

Rainfall is normally measured just once a day, usually at 9am. You can make a daily rainfall chart, or you can add up each day's rainfall to give a monthly total and draw a chart for the year. Most rainfall charts are yearly charts.

The best way to plot rainfall is to use a column chart. Picture ④ shows what a rainfall chart might look like for one year.

This is what the water collected in raingauge bottles for each month of the year would look like if the 12 bottles were placed side by side.

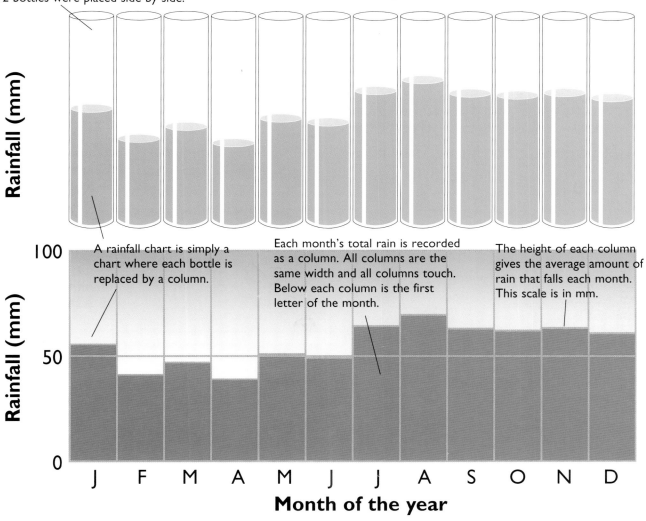

A rainfall chart is simply a chart where each bottle is replaced by a column.

Each month's total rain is recorded as a column. All columns are the same width and all columns touch. Below each column is the first letter of the month.

The height of each column gives the average amount of rain that falls each month. This scale is in mm.

Rainfall (mm)

Month of the year

▲ ④ This is what a yearly rainfall chart looks like for Edinburgh, Scotland. The chart shows the average rainfall for each month. Notice that there is not much difference between months, although Spring is slightly drier than other times of the year.

By the way… Snow depth is measured with a ruler pushed through the snow to the ground. About 12 cm of freshly fallen snow contains the same water as 1 cm of rainfall.

Rainy seasons

In many tropical countries it is warm all the year, but rain falls only in certain months. As a result, many tropical places call their seasons by the amount of rain that falls.

Whereas people in the mid-latitudes describe their seasons by temperature changes (Summer, Autumn, Winter and Spring), there is little change of temperature in the **TROPICS**, and so the people who live there cannot use this way of talking about seasons.

However, in many tropical places enormous amounts of rain fall at certain times of the year, while at other times there is no rain at all. As a result, many people in the Tropics describe their seasons by rainfall, calling them **WET** (rainy) and **DRY SEASONS**.

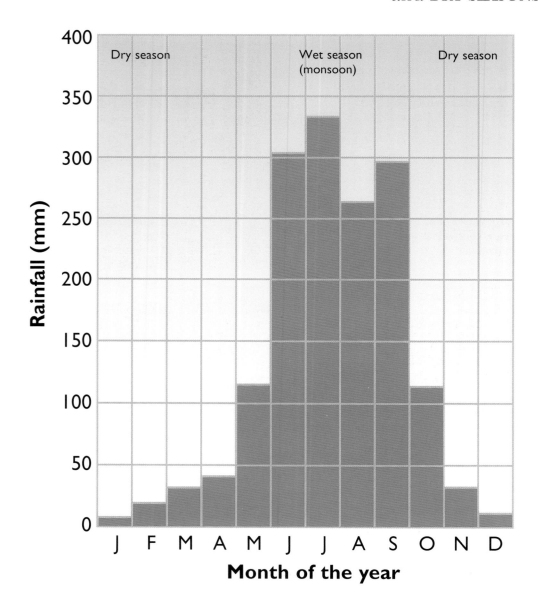

◄ ① This is the rainfall chart for Calcutta, India. You should always look at a rainfall chart from a distance first. This way you can look at the shape. In this chart you will see that some columns are much taller than others. The tall columns show the rainy season. Some of the columns are very short; this is the dry season.

You can see how seasons work in the Tropics by looking at tropical Asia. The chart shows the rainfall in Calcutta, India (picture ①). You can see that, between June and September, a very large amount of rain falls. This is the rainy season. By October, very little rain falls, and the Sun shines almost every day for many months. This is the dry season. Pictures ② to ⑥ on this page show you what the weather is like in tropical Asia.

◀ ④ It can be very miserable in the wet season, as shown by this picture from Thailand. See how the sky is grey and mist clings to the tree-tops.

▼ ⑤ Without rain, the forests become parched and widespread forest fires are common. This is Thailand in the dry season.

◀ ② During the wet season the streets of Calcutta are almost permanently wet, and flooding is common. (Notice that many people are wearing shorts, because it is warm throughout the year in the Tropics.)

▼ ③ The wet season provides the water that is needed for rice to grow in paddy fields, as here in Bali, Indonesia.

▲ ⑥ Crops ripen after the rainy season and are harvested. The grass stops growing, making it difficult to feed animals. See how bare the ground is in the background. This is India in the dry season.

Wind

Breezes, winds, gales and hurricanes are all forms of air on the move.

The air all around us is made of gases. We don't see them, but when they move we can feel them as winds.

Measuring the wind

Wind has both strength and direction. The simplest way to measure the wind direction is with a **WIND VANE** (picture ①). The wind turns the flat surface of the vane edge-on to the wind, with the (smaller) pointed end facing into the wind.

A **WIND SOCK** is a tube of fabric tied to a mast (picture ②). The end of the tube is held open by a wire ring. When the wind blows, the sock fills with air and starts to rise. The stronger the wind, the higher the end of the wind sock lifts. The open end of the sock points into the wind.

An instrument called an **ANEMOMETER** is used to measure wind speed accurately. It is made of three little cups on a rod (picture ①). The cups catch the wind and cause the rod to spin. An electrical device records the spin to show the wind speed.

▼ ① A wind vane and anemometer are often mounted together as part of an electronic weather centre. Leads from each instrument go to a computer that shows the wind speed and direction.

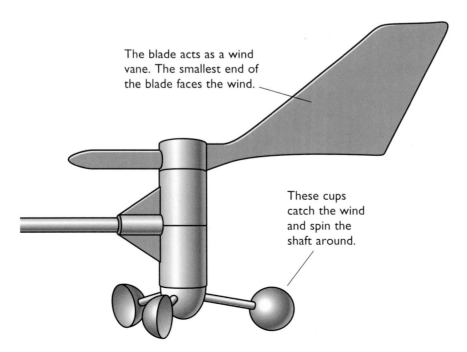

The blade acts as a wind vane. The smallest end of the blade faces the wind.

These cups catch the wind and spin the shaft around.

▼ ② The strength of the wind can easily be seen using a wind sock. To make a wind sock like the one shown below, you need a tube of lightweight material, such as nylon, a piece of wire and a stick.

Make a circle of wire to keep the end of the sock open and stitch the sock to the wire. Tie the sock to a stick using a loop of string, as in the picture.

When the wind blows, the wind sock will fill with air and rise clear of the stick: the stronger the wind, the higher the end will rise. The foot end of the sock will point away from the wind.

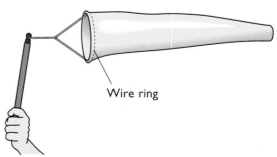

Wire ring

A wind scale

Not everyone has an instrument for measuring wind speed. Many years ago a wind scale was developed for the Navy by Admiral Beaufort. The **BEAUFORT SCALE,** shown below, was named after him. Notice that it uses simple observations to give an idea of wind speed (picture ③).

Looking at trees and plants

Plants and trees can tell you what the wind is like, on average. Where strong winds commonly blow from the same direction (known as **PREVAILING WINDS**), plants turn away to protect themselves. Check this out on hilly land or by the seaside.

▼ ③ The Beaufort scale

0

Calm
Calm; smoke rises vertically

1

Light air
Direction of wind shown by smoke drift, but not by wind vanes.

2

Light breeze
Wind felt on face; leaves rustle; ordinary vane moved by wind.

3

Gentle breeze
Leaves and small twigs in constant motion; wind extends light flag.

4

Moderate breeze
Raises dust and loose paper; small branches are moved.

5

Fresh breeze
Small trees in leaf begin to sway; crested wavelets form on inland waters.

6

Strong breeze
Large branches in motion; whistling heard in telegraph wires; umbrellas used with difficulty.

7

Near gale
Whole trees in motion; inconvenience felt when walking against the wind.

8

Gale
Breaks twigs off trees; generally impedes progress.

9

Strong gale
Slight structural damage occurs (chimney pots and slates removed).

10

Storm
Seldom experienced inland; trees uprooted; considerable structural damage occurs.

11

Violent storm
Very rarely experienced; accompanied by widespread damage.

12

Hurricane
Severe damage.

How 'bubbling' clouds are made

Hot air rises whether it is moist or not, but rising moist air quickly makes clouds with a bubbling shape.

Watching a hot-air balloon rising helps us to understand how some clouds are formed. The gas burner in the basket heats the air inside the balloon, and the balloon rises silently into the air (picture ①).

If the burner is turned off, the balloon keeps rising for a while, but soon the air in the balloon gets cold and the balloon stops rising.

Hot air inside a balloon makes the balloon rise because hot air is much lighter – less dense – than the cold air around it.

◀ ① Gas burners heating the air in a hot-air balloon

▼ ② This extraordinary picture shows air rising from the towers of a power station. The air coming from the towers is very hot and very moist. It rises quickly and reaches great heights. As it rises it cools and moisture turns into droplets. As a result, you see the path of the rising air as a plume of cloud.

When the burner is turned off, the air in the balloon quickly shares its heat with the surrounding atmosphere, and cools down. Once it is the same temperature as the surroundings, it is no longer lighter, and it stops rising. Most clouds have a 'life' of between 20 minutes to a couple of hours.

Why bubbling clouds form

Bubbling – or CUMULUS – clouds are formed when air is warmed from below (picture ②). The warmed air becomes lighter than the air above, and begins to rise.

▼ ③ **This diagram shows how cumulus clouds can be formed. It may help to imagine air bubbles as though they were many invisible hot air balloons rising one after another.**

A cloud produced in this way has a short life, but more air is being warmed and new bubbles are rising all the time to replace the bubbles that have finished their lives.

Why we see clouds

Clouds are made of <u>moist</u>, warm air. Dry air will not form clouds. When a moist air bubble cools enough, the water vapour in it changes to droplets and you see the rising air bubble as a cloud (picture ③).

3 As the rising bubble rises, it cools and can hold less and less vapour.
   Finally, some vapour is converted into millions of tiny droplets of water. Now we can see the bubble for the first time, and we call it a cloud.

2 Not all the heated air can rise at the same time, so 'bubbles' of it rise. You can't see them because they are invisible, but glider pilots and birds use them to keep aloft. Pilots call these rising air currents THERMALS.

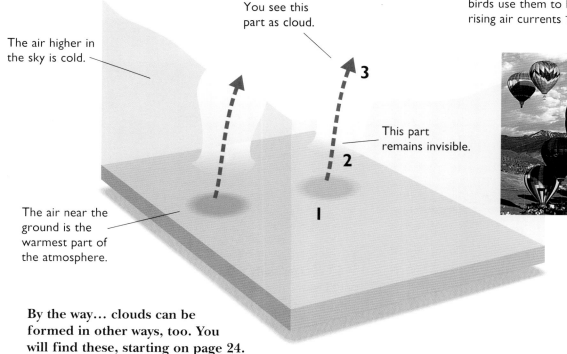

You see this part as cloud.

The air higher in the sky is cold.

3

This part remains invisible.

2

The air near the ground is the warmest part of the atmosphere.

1

1 On a warm day the sun heats the ground. The warm ground shares its heat with the air above (this is just like the burner in the balloon).

By the way… clouds can be formed in other ways, too. You will find these, starting on page 24.

Clouds with a daily routine

Cumulus clouds form when warm, moist air rises. When the weather is hot, they follow a daily pattern.

If the day starts clear and sunny, then cumulus clouds can be expected to form. The clear sky allows the sunshine to warm the ground. Soon the ground shares its heat with the air, and bubbles of warmed air begin to rise. At first, the air is not very warm and only small bubbles form. But during the morning, as the ground becomes warmer and the air is heated more strongly, the bubbles get bigger and then great towering cumulus clouds may begin to cover the sky (picture ①).

As the Sun goes down and the ground is heated less, so the clouds finally fade away (picture ②).

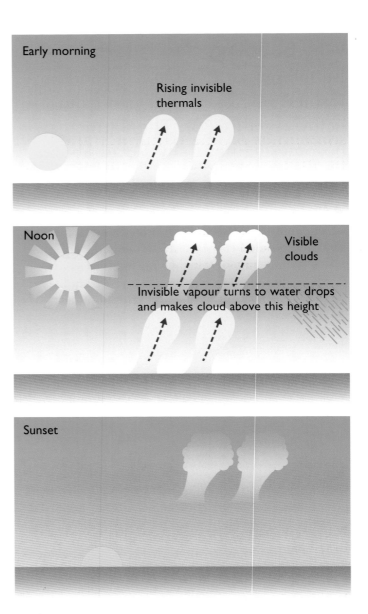

▲ ② The daily pattern of cumulus clouds.
These diagrams show you how cumulus clouds grow in the morning, cover the sky and produce heavy showers during the afternoon, and then fade away by evening. This is a daily, or DIURNAL, pattern common in many parts of the world.

▲ ① These impressive cumulus clouds are in the tropics, where the sea gives a lot of moisture to the air. Strong tropical heating produces towering clouds and torrential rain, or even HAIL, each day.

Rain clouds

Cumulus clouds do not all grow to be giants. Sometimes the air simply never gets hot enough, or there is not enough moisture to make droplets. These smaller, cumulus clouds are sometimes called 'cotton wool clouds'. Normally they tell of fine weather.

Only the biggest cumulus clouds produce rain (picture ③). These are the ones with dark undersides. Giant cumulus clouds form only when the air is hot and humid. They can sometimes produce thunder and lightning (see page 24) (picture ④).

▼ ③ You can see rain is pouring out of the bottom of this dark cloud. These clouds are called cumulonimbus clouds, which means 'rain-bearing' cumulus.

▶ ④ The shape of the top of this giant cloud shows clearly that bubbles of moist air are pushing up higher and higher all the time.

Thunder and lightning

The biggest cumulus clouds produce some of the most spectacular displays to be seen in the sky.

Giant cumulus clouds are the tallest clouds in the sky. They have fearsome winds within them that can cause thunder and lightning, as well as tornadoes (see page 38).

Thunderclouds form most often after a day of hot, muggy weather. The air feels muggy because it is so full of moisture. Hot air can hold more moisture than cool air and contains a huge amount of energy.

This energy will eventually produce thunder and lightning.

How lightning is produced

LIGHTNING is a natural spark of static electricity. This sort of electricity is produced when one object brushes quickly against another. You can make sparks jump from your clothing by rubbing a plastic comb against

▼ ① **This diagram shows a side view through a thundercloud.**

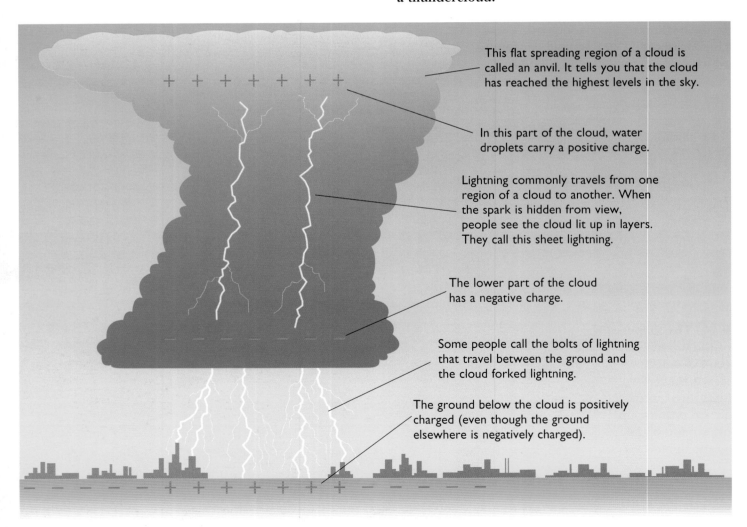

This flat spreading region of a cloud is called an anvil. It tells you that the cloud has reached the highest levels in the sky.

In this part of the cloud, water droplets carry a positive charge.

Lightning commonly travels from one region of a cloud to another. When the spark is hidden from view, people see the cloud lit up in layers. They call this sheet lightning.

The lower part of the cloud has a negative charge.

Some people call the bolts of lightning that travel between the ground and the cloud forked lightning.

The ground below the cloud is positively charged (even though the ground elsewhere is negatively charged).

your clothes very quickly, and then holding the comb a little way from your hand.

In the thundercloud the heat in the air gives the energy for bubbles of air to rise very, very fast (picture ①). The rising air drags countless water droplets with it. Static electricity is produced when these droplets are whisked quickly through the air by gusts of wind inside the cloud.

Opposite charges are needed for a spark. Lightning sometimes jumps from the bottom of the cloud to the ground, or from the bottom of the cloud to the cloud top.

▲ ② **This spectacular picture shows many 'bolts' of lightning travelling between the base of the cloud and the ground. Lightning is attracted to upright objects such as trees, telegraph poles or tall buildings.**

People are at risk if they stand out in the open, or continue to use a swimming pool. By contrast, people inside cars are perfectly safe from lightning.

Thunder

As the spark jumps, it heats the air around it (picture ②). The air expands so fast that it sets up shock waves in the air. The shock waves are heard as **THUNDER**. To find out how far a cloud is from you, count the time in seconds from seeing the lightning to hearing the rumble of thunder. This number is the same as the distance to the cloud in miles.

Clouds in layers

Many clouds form as widespread sheets or layers that give long periods of drizzle or light rain.

When the sky is overcast and dull, there are layer clouds above you. These clouds are very common and stretch right across the sky. But there is more variety than you might have noticed (picture ①). Each type of layer cloud is given its own name. Here are some of them.

The highest layer cloud is called **CIRRUS**. Cirrus contains ice crystals (snowflakes).

STRATUS clouds are lower and contain water droplets. These are often the clouds that bring dull or overcast weather and long periods of rain.

▼ ① Layer clouds are given names that tell you how thick and high they are and whether they are made of raindrops or snowflakes. Note that this pattern of clouds is common at a WEATHER FRONT. Weather fronts are described on page 30.

Wisps of cloud occur only very high in the sky. Their fuzzy shape tells that they are made of snowflakes. They are too thin to produce rain. They are called cirrus clouds (meaning wispy clouds).

Thin layer clouds allow the sun to shine through. They are too thin to produce rain. They are called **ALTOSTRATUS** clouds (meaning medium height layer clouds).

Thick, low layer clouds produce widespread rain. They are called nimbostratus clouds (meaning 'rain-bearing' layer clouds).

WARM AIR

COLD AIR

How layer clouds are formed

Layer clouds are formed in a very different way from the bubbling cumulus clouds described on page 20. No hot ground is needed for layer clouds to form, just a way of pushing air upwards, so that it all cools and makes droplets at the same time.

The easiest way to understand how layer clouds form is first to look at the clouds surrounding mountains. As wind blows air against mountains, the moist air is forced up and over them (picture ②). As the air rises, it cools and makes clouds (picture ③).

Many layer clouds form in areas where there are no mountains. When you see this, you know that there are two different kinds of air in the sky above (picture ①). One part of the sky will have air that is slightly warmer than the other. The wind pushes these different kinds of air together. The colder air is heavier than the warm air, so the cold air hugs the ground and the warm air is pushed over it. We can't see this until the warm air is lifted so high that it forms thick sheets of clouds. The region where cool air meets warm air is called a **WEATHER FRONT**. Fronts are described on page 30.

▲ ③ **This picture shows clouds forming as air is lifted over a range of hills. The bottom of the cloud shows the height at which the air is cooled enough to change moisture into water droplets.**

▼ ② **This diagram shows the effects of mountains on clouds.**

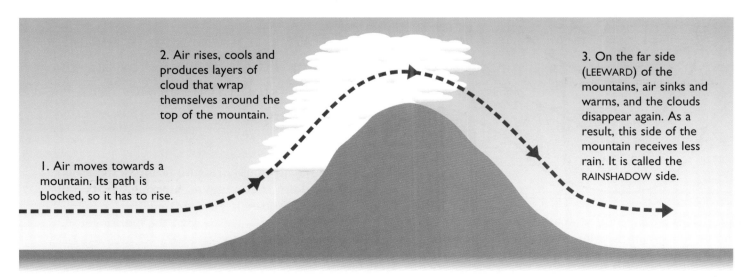

2. Air rises, cools and produces layers of cloud that wrap themselves around the top of the mountain.

3. On the far side (LEEWARD) of the mountains, air sinks and warms, and the clouds disappear again. As a result, this side of the mountain receives less rain. It is called the RAINSHADOW side.

I. Air moves towards a mountain. Its path is blocked, so it has to rise.

Settled weather

Settled weather occurs when air is still. In summer this gives hot sunny days, but in winter it gives cold weather and sometimes fog.

Have you ever noticed that sometimes the weather is very 'settled', while at other times it is very changeable? These changes give many of us the variety in our weather and it is the weather forecaster's job to foresee the patterns ahead. To do this, the forecaster needs to use two key words – **HIGH PRESSURE,** or **ANTICYCLONE,** and **LOW PRESSURE,** or **DEPRESSION**. In general, high pressure means settled, dry weather, and low pressure means changeable, rainy weather. The causes of settled weather can be seen here; you will find the causes of changeable weather on page 30.

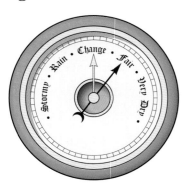

▶ ② A BAROMETER measures the pressure of the air. When the needle points to 'fair' or moves to the right, this tells of a high pressure.

Signs of settled weather

The tell-tale signs of settled weather are shown on a weather forecaster's map by the word **HIGH** (picture ①).

You can spot a high pressure even without a weather map. In summer, settled weather gives bright, sunny days with no more than small 'fair weather' cumulus clouds scattered across the sky (picture ③). Winter skies may also be fine and clear with pink and purple sunsets (picture ④). **FOG** is common overnight (picture ⑤).

HAZE is another sign of settled weather. Haze occurs as the air fills with dust and prevents you from seeing long distances.

▲ ① This is what settled weather looks like on TV and on newspaper weather maps. Notice the word **HIGH**. The rings (called ISOBARS) give an idea of how windy it is: few rings – as here – are a sign of light winds. There are no weather fronts in a high.

By the way… A high pressure occurs when air is settling down over a region, pressing down on the ground and squashing the air together, so increasing the AIR PRESSURE. This is what the barometer measures (picture ②).

The settling air stops most warm air bubbles rising. As a result there is often no cloud at all, even though the ground may be scorching hot.

◄ ③ In settled weather the sky may be clear, or small cumulus clouds may form. They do not grow, and so no rain can fall. This is why they are called 'fair-weather cumulus' clouds.

▲ ⑤ In settled weather the sky is clear overnight and so the air loses heat. Moist air, such as is found near lakes and rivers, can easily form overnight fog. This is then 'burned off' by the heat of the next day.

◄▲ ④ Red sunset in summer (above), and pink and purple colours at sunset in winter (left) tell of settled weather.

Changeable weather

**Why does the weather change quickly in many parts of the world?
The answer is usually connected with a weather front.**

The tell-tale sign of changeable weather on a weather forecaster's map is the word **LOW** (picture ①). A barometer needle will also move to 'change' (picture ②).

A low is the opposite to a high. In a low, air is swirling upwards and lifting off of the ground (picture ③). This makes it easy for clouds to form even when there is no sun to warm the ground.

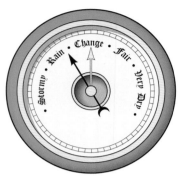

◄ ② Barometer points to 'change', or moves to the left.

Changeable sky

Unlike settled weather, the changeable sky is filled with cloud, usually sheets of layer cloud (picture ④).

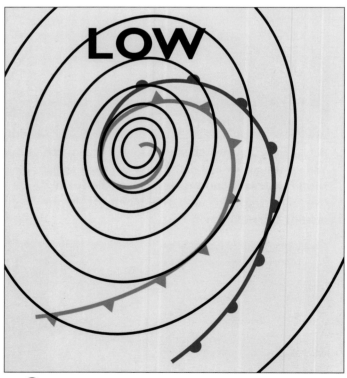

▲ ① This is what changeable weather looks like on weather maps: there are lots of rings (isobars) that tell of windier weather and the word **LOW** in the centre. The fronts are marked by red and blue lines. This is where it is most likely to rain. The warm front is shown by a red line and the cold front is shown by a blue line.

▲ ③ This is a satellite picture of the map. You can clearly see the great swirl of cloud.

Forecasters use the word **FRONT** to show places where the main sheets of cloud form. The first sign of a front is a thin sheet of cloud high in the sky. This is cirrus cloud (picture ⑤).

Over the next few hours, the clouds will be lower, thicker and darker. These are stratus clouds. People call this an **OVERCAST SKY**. (Finally the cloud will be thick enough to make rain.)

Rain does not always fall, but all fronts are marked by overcast skies. Fronts mainly occur in pairs. When the sky brightens and the cloud breaks up, you know that the fronts have passed.

▼ ④ When a front is overhead, this is what you see. There are many layers of cloud above you. Together, they keep out most of the sunlight, and this is why they look dark.

▼ ⑤ This is what a side view through a low looks like. Notice thick heaps of cloud marking each front. Most lows have two fronts; the one on the right is called a warm front because warm air follows behind it; the one on the left is called a cold front because cold air follows behind it.

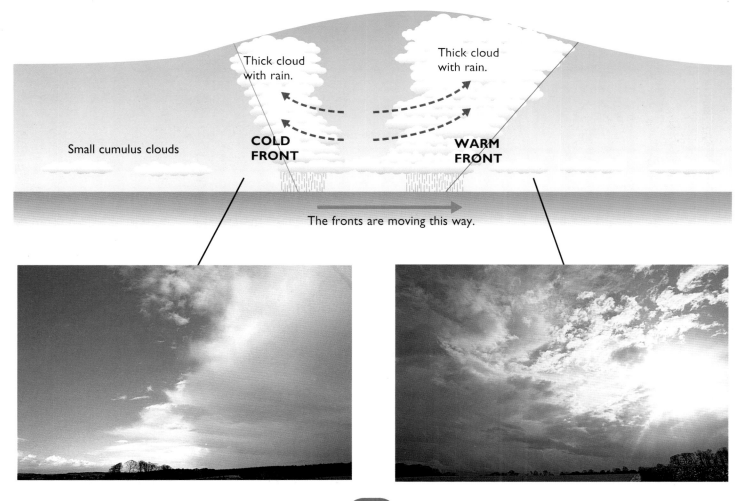

Thick cloud with rain.

Thick cloud with rain.

Small cumulus clouds

COLD FRONT

WARM FRONT

The fronts are moving this way.

Hill and valley weather

Air rises and sinks in valleys, giving hills and valleys their own special weather.

When there is little wind, the weather can be affected by the local shape of the land, nearness to the sea or the presence of large cities. These all give rise to **LOCAL WEATHER**.

Shady and sunny valleys

In places with steep-sided valleys, one side of a valley can stay in shadow for much longer than the other side (picture ①).

The shady side of a valley stays much colder than the sunlit side.

▼ ① This diagram shows how the rising Sun warms one side of a valley faster than the other.

This is more important in winter, when the sun is always low in the sky.

Crops, such as grapes, will ripen better on the sunny slopes than on the shady slopes.

People prefer to live on the warmer, sunny side rather than on the colder, shady side. This is one reason why villages and towns are often found only on the sunny sides of deep valleys.

Frost pockets

During the night the ground loses heat to the atmosphere, and the air close to the ground cools down.

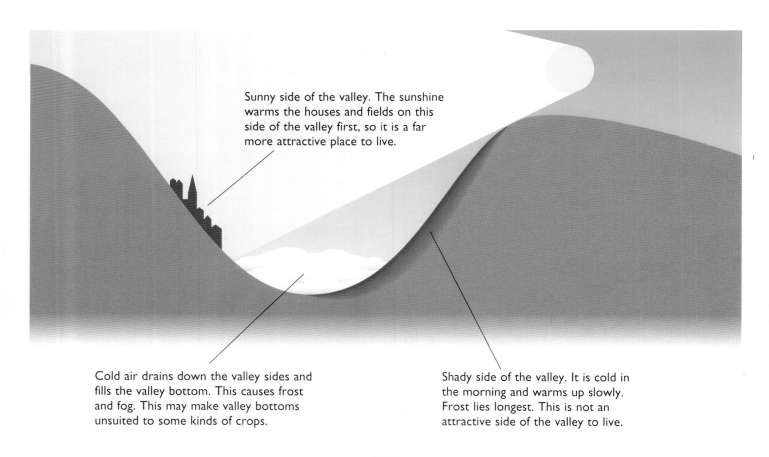

Sunny side of the valley. The sunshine warms the houses and fields on this side of the valley first, so it is a far more attractive place to live.

Cold air drains down the valley sides and fills the valley bottom. This causes frost and fog. This may make valley bottoms unsuited to some kinds of crops.

Shady side of the valley. It is cold in the morning and warms up slowly. Frost lies longest. This is not an attractive side of the valley to live.

Cold air is heavier than warm air and it rolls down hillsides, producing a night-time breeze.

When the cold air gets to the valley floor, it has nowhere else to go, so it builds up, often causing frost (picture ②) and fog, especially where there is plenty of moisture such as above rivers and lakes (see also picture ①, page 12).

Pollution traps

Valleys trap air, but they also trap pollution. This means that factories sited in valleys often make the air around them heavily polluted (picture ③).

Snowy passes

The higher you are, the colder it is. During winter many high valleys, especially mountain passes, receive snow instead of rain and the snow does not melt because the air is too cold (picture ④).

◀ ② Frosty valley floors may make life harder for animals.

▲ ③ Valleys in mountain regions are very sheltered places. See how the pollution from this factory is filling the valley bottom, rather than being blown away.

◀ ④ This picture shows snow still being cleared from a mountain pass in early summer.

Routes between mountainous areas can be blocked by snow for several months during winter.

Weather at the coast

The weather at the coast is often very different from that just a short distance inland. This is due to breezes blowing on and off the shore.

The sea changes temperature very slowly through the seasons. In contrast, the land heats up and cools down quickly, both from day to day and through the seasons. Here are some of the effects.

Sea breezes

The air over the sea is always moist. For at least part of the year the sea itself is cooler than the air. During the day the Sun heats the land which, in turn, heats the air above it. This warmed air rises, pulling the cooler air in off the sea, thus creating a cool **SEA BREEZE** (picture ①). This is why, when the land is hot, coasts are often the coolest places (picture ②).

Coastal fog

Coastal fog is produced when warm, moist air blows over cold sea waters. As the air flows over the sea, it is cooled, causing some of the water vapour to turn into droplets. These droplets form fog above the sea which can also stretch onto the nearby land.

Coastal fog can also disappear quickly. The three pictures shown opposite (picture ③) were taken within five minutes of each other. The fog was 'burned off' by the heat of a summer Sun warming the air from above, turning the droplets back into vapour.

▼ ① This diagram shows the way in which a sea breeze is produced. Notice that the breeze is set up because the land is warmed, causing the warmed air to rise. Cool air flows in from the sea to take the place of the rising warm air. This is an example of CONVECTION.

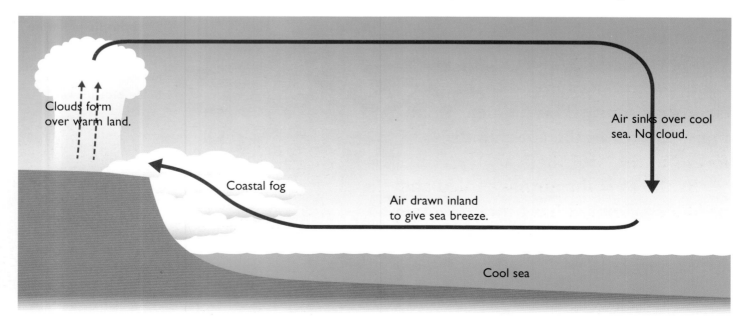

Clouds form over warm land.

Coastal fog

Air sinks over cool sea. No cloud.

Air drawn inland to give sea breeze.

Cool sea

◀ ② There is usually a pleasant breeze on a beach, even on a scorching-hot, sunny day. This is because air is being drawn inland over a cooler sea. Notice the clouds bubbling up inland, well away from the coast.

▼ ③ When the fog is not very dense, the heat from the Sun can warm the air and 'burn off' the fog. These three pictures of a coast were taken within 5 minutes of each other at about 11am. You can see the cloud thinning (left to right). The fog lasts longest in the estuary where the river water is cold.

Coast cloud

Widespread cloud often occurs just inland of the coast even though the coast stays sunny. This happens when moist air crosses the coast and is forced to rise over the land.

By the time the air has cooled and produced cloud, it has travelled some distance inland, and so the coast stays clear (picture ③).

▲ ③ This picture shows cloud forming just inland of the coast. The air is flowing from right to left. Notice how the coast remains sunny and clear. This pattern is the result of a sea breeze.

City weather

Cities store and give out heat. The bigger the city and the more densely packed its streets, the more the weather differs from that in the surrounding countryside.

City heat island

City centres are usually warmer than the nearby suburbs, which, in turn are warmer than the nearby countryside. This can make them more pleasant in winter, but more stifling in summer.

The extra warmth in a city is caused by two things. Firstly, the buildings are heated in winter and this heat seeps out into the surrounding air. Secondly, the centre of a city has densely packed buildings that shelter the streets from strong winds, and trap warm air (picture ①).

For these reasons city centres tend to be the warmest places, while the suburbs, with their large areas of gardens and well-spaced houses, tend to be only slightly warmer than the countryside.

Geographers call the warmer air in a city a **HEAT ISLAND**, because it is a small, warmer 'island' in a 'sea' of cooler countryside (picture ②). Early Springs and late Autumns are experienced in cities (picture ③).

▼ ② **If you could see the air over a city, and if its colour showed how warm it is, this is what you might see! The air is warmer above the city centre, cooler in the suburbs and coolest in the open country. The symbols of thermometers show the heat island in side view and as a plan.**

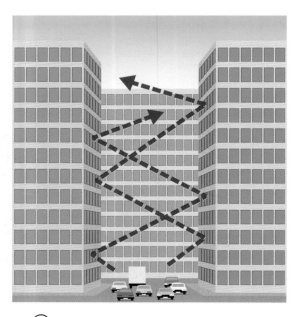

▲ ① Here you can see how heat bounces back and forth between buildings, keeping city streets warmer than elsewhere.

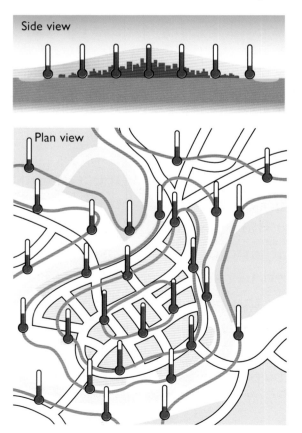

▶ ③ Spring comes sooner, and Autumn lasts longer, in a city because the buildings keep it more sheltered and warmer. You notice this in the parks, where the flowers come out sooner and the trees stay in leaf longer.

City pollution

Cities can also change the local weather because of the gases they send into the air. Car fumes contain many gases, as do fumes from power stations, factories, and so on.

Some of these gases combine with strong sunlight to make a kind of yellow–brown haze, known as **SMOG** (picture ④).

The gases can also be carried high into the air; here they mix with cloud droplets, forming acids. When rain falls from clouds like these, it is called **ACID RAIN**.

▶ ④ A yellow–brown pollution called smog hangs over some cities such as Los Angeles and Mexico City. It is especially bad in places which are built in basins surrounded by mountains, because here the air gets trapped and breezes are uncommon.

These pictures show Mexico City during a long, dry spell and after rain when the pollutants have just been washed out of the air. Notice that, when the air is polluted, you cannot even see the mountains in the distance.

Tornadoes

The world's fiercest winds occur in tornadoes. Although they last for just a few minutes, they can destroy houses and even lift cars and trains into the air.

A **TORNADO** comes from the Spanish *tronada*, or thunderstorm. Tornadoes are tightly spinning, funnel-shaped clouds that appear to hang from the bottom of a thundercloud (picture ①).

The winds in the centre of the funnel are the fastest in the world, some reaching 800 km/hr. They quickly pass over the ground, but the destruction they can cause in just a few minutes' passage can be tremendous (picture ②).

The size of a tornado

Tornadoes are produced as air is sucked very quickly into the bottom of a thunderstorm. They can form over land or water (where they are called **WATERSPOUTS**).

Tornadoes may be just a few tens of metres across where they touch the ground; the biggest are only some hundreds of metres across (picture ③). They may last for less than an hour, and may travel just a few tens of kilometres.

▼ ① These are the main features of a tornado.

The air spins violently in the funnel, which is why tornadoes are also given the nickname 'TWISTER'.

Air flows into the bottom of the funnel very quickly, sucking up buildings, trees, locomotives, cars and anything else that is in its path.

Funnel cloud writhes about, connecting the ground to the bottom of the thundercloud.

Intense rain falls from a tornado-bearing thunderstorm; thunder and lightning are also common.

Strong wind blows ahead of the tornado.

▲ ② This tornado is clearly picking up enormous amounts of soil from the land, causing the funnel to turn black. The telegraph poles give the scale.

▶ ③ Here you can see the close relationship between a tornado and a thunderstorm. Notice the lightning behind the tornado funnel.

Inside a tornado the air is very 'thin' (it is an area of very low pressure). Many buildings that have been tightly shuttered for protection often explode as a tornado passes because the air pressure inside the building remains much greater than that on the outside.

Tornadoes are very much smaller than tropical cyclones (hurricanes), but because tropical cyclones have great walls of thunderclouds inside them, tornadoes often occur with hurricanes.

Tornadoes are encountered widely, from the cool lands of the United Kingdom to the warmer areas of Australia, but they are by far the most common in the United States, which holds the world record at an average of 1000 each year, most wreaking havoc between May and July.

By the way... small tornado-like areas of spinning air are called WHIRLWINDS.

The scale of severity of tornadoes

Scale	Wind speed	Expected damage
F-0	70–109 km/hr	Slight damage
F-1	110–179 km/hr	Moderate damage
F-2	180–249 km/hr	Considerable damage
F-3	250–329 km/hr	Severe damage
F-4	330–414 km/hr	Devastating damage
F-5	over 415 km/hr	Incredible damage

Tropical cyclones

Tropical cyclones, also called hurricanes or typhoons, are spirals of air from which torrential rain falls and the wind blows at more than 117 km/hr. Their winds can destroy houses and also can cause the sea to surge inland.

Tropical cyclones are called **HURRICANES** in the Atlantic and Eastern Pacific (from the West Indian word *hurrican,* meaning big wind) and **TYPHOONS** in the Western Pacific (from the Chinese *taifun* which means great wind).

Hurricane-force winds can uproot trees, demolish houses and leave a trail of death and destruction. Some of these winds may travel at the speed of a bullet – and do far more damage.

What is a tropical cyclone?

Tropical cyclones are vast, swirling masses of cloud that mainly (but not always) move within and near the Tropics. They may travel many thousands of kilometres and they may last for weeks (picture ①).

Tropical cyclones form only over oceans warmer than 27°C (80°F). The hot ocean waters send heat and enormous amounts of moisture directly to the lowest levels of the air above. Once heated, the hot, moist air then rises quickly.

As the air rises, it cools and can no longer hold all of the moisture as vapour. The moisture starts to turn back into water droplets, producing huge walls of cloud and releasing

▲ ① This is a tropical cyclone seen from space. Compare it with the cross-section opposite.

torrential rain and heat energy (picture ②). The heat causes the air to rise faster still, and the clouds grow even bigger.

The rising air soon begins to spin around a calm, often clear and sunny centre, called the **EYE** (picture ③).

Cyclones die away only when they pass over cold ocean water or cold land, so that the supply of hot, moist air is then cut off.

► ② This is a cross-section of a hurricane. Notice that the clouds are caught in the spiralling winds. The eye is in the centre. The fiercest winds occur at the edge of the eye, a place called the eye-wall.

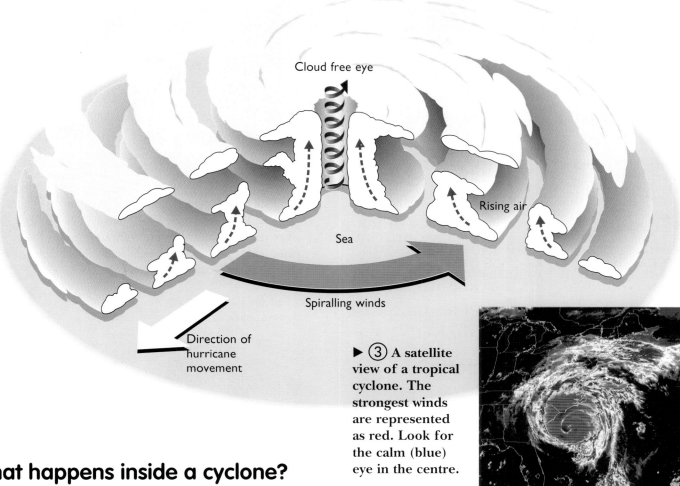

Cloud free eye

Rising air

Sea

Spiralling winds

Direction of hurricane movement

► ③ A satellite view of a tropical cyclone. The strongest winds are represented as red. Look for the calm (blue) eye in the centre.

What happens inside a cyclone?

Think of a tropical cyclone as a spinning top. The top spins furiously <u>and</u> wobbles in a curving path. The winds inside the tropical cyclone may be going at over 117 km/hr, whilst the whole cyclone moves across the ocean at perhaps 12 km/hr, faster as it moves away from the tropics.

Because a tropical cyclone may be over 800 km across, a cyclone moving at 12 km/hr would affect an area for two days, with the most severe and damaging winds lasting for about 12 hours.

Storm surge

Nine out of every ten people killed by tropical storms are drowned. This is because tropical cyclones are very low pressure areas, so water rises inside them. The level of the sea beneath a tropical cyclone may be 10 m or more above normal. This very high water may be blown onshore. This is called a **STORM SURGE**. It occurs without warning and drowns many people who remain on low-lying coasts.

A world of climates

The long-term weather, or climate, that people experience is different across the world.

Whereas the weather is what it is like from day to day, the climate is what it is like <u>on average</u>.

The effect of temperature

The climate is not the same everywhere. The Earth heats up most in the Tropics, because here the Sun shines overhead every day; it is much colder near the poles where the Sun rises to only a low angle in the sky and as a result heats the ground least (picture ①).

This is why the world's climate is divided into temperature bands, each roughly parallel with the Equator (picture ②).

▼ ① **This diagram shows you the way in which the winds move across the Earth. Hot air rises over the Equator, and cold air sinks over the poles. Hot and cold air mix in the mid-latitudes to give changeable weather.**

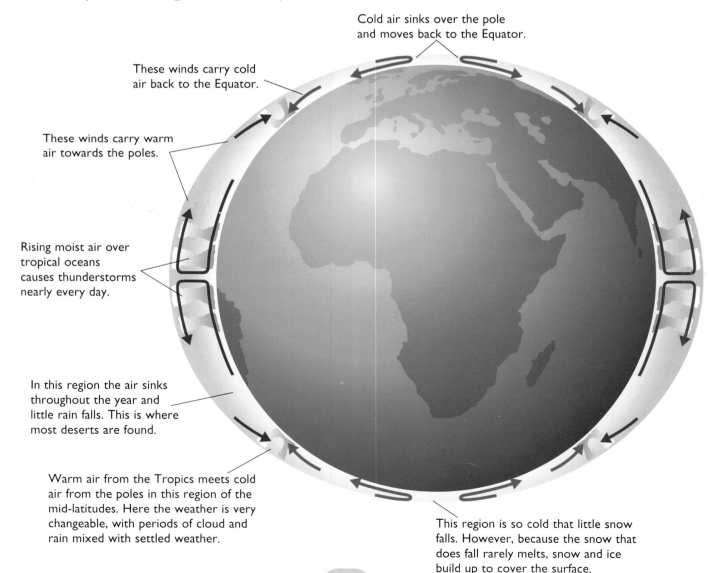

Cold air sinks over the pole and moves back to the Equator.

These winds carry cold air back to the Equator.

These winds carry warm air towards the poles.

Rising moist air over tropical oceans causes thunderstorms nearly every day.

In this region the air sinks throughout the year and little rain falls. This is where most deserts are found.

Warm air from the Tropics meets cold air from the poles in this region of the mid-latitudes. Here the weather is very changeable, with periods of cloud and rain mixed with settled weather.

This region is so cold that little snow falls. However, because the snow that does fall rarely melts, snow and ice build up to cover the surface.

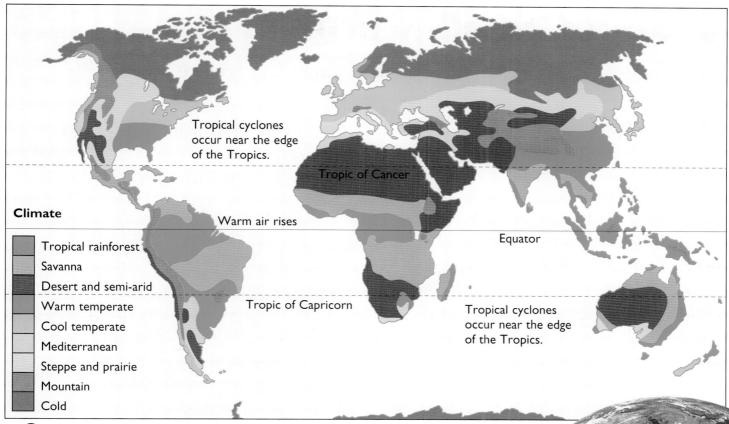

Climate

- Tropical rainforest
- Savanna
- Desert and semi-arid
- Warm temperate
- Cool temperate
- Mediterranean
- Steppe and prairie
- Mountain
- Cold

Tropical cyclones occur near the edge of the Tropics.

Tropic of Cancer

Warm air rises

Equator

Tropic of Capricorn

Tropical cyclones occur near the edge of the Tropics.

▲ ② This map shows the main types of climate across the earth. Notice how the climates are mainly laid out in bands parallel to the Equator. Mountains and other special features break up the pattern.

▶ ③ A satellite picture of Earth from space shows Africa with clouds over the equator (centre) and clear skies over the deserts (top).

The effect of rainfall

Rain occurs only with moist air. The biggest sources of moisture are the oceans. As a result, where there are moist onshore winds, there are wet climates. Places far from oceans or places where winds blow offshore have much drier climates. Places with heavy rainfall are said to have **MARITIME CLIMATES**, whereas drier places are said to have **CONTINENTAL CLIMATES**.

Special climates

In some parts of the world there are areas that have special climates. The land that lies in the shelter of mountains are known as rainshadow zones (see page 27). Here you find many of the world's **DESERTS** (picture ③).

Another special climate is called a **MONSOON**. This is most pronounced over India. Each June the dry season changes to the wet season (the monsoon) very abruptly.

Change: global warming and El Niño

Two weather events affect everyone in the world: global warming and El Niño.

Global warming

All of the heat that we receive from the Sun is gradually lost back to space. In this way the Earth doesn't naturally get hotter or colder.

What change means

Over the past centuries, burning coal and oil, or burning up forests, have added to the amount of carbon dioxide gas in the air. Carbon dioxide can trap heat (picture ①). As a result the temperature of the air has been rising in many places (picture ②). This is called GLOBAL WARMING.

The warming has already caused ice sheets to begin to melt in the Arctic and Antarctic. The water has caused sea levels to rise up to 25 cm, and further rises are sure to happen. This will cause low-lying coastal areas to flood in the near future.

Diseases that occur today only in the Tropics may become more widespread. Some places will get too hot and dry to grow crops, and there may not be enough drinking water.

The only way to make global warming less severe is to reduce the amount of carbon dioxide in the air, which means burning less fuel (picture ③). We can act now, while the problem appears small, to save the world's people from disastrous weather changes in the future.

◄ ① Carbon dioxide traps some of the heat that would otherwise be lost to space. The more carbon dioxide there is in the air, the more heat is trapped. The extra heat stored in the air is often called the GREENHOUSE EFFECT.

▲ ② This map shows which places seem to be getting hotter and which seem to be getting colder due to global warming. What is happening where you live?

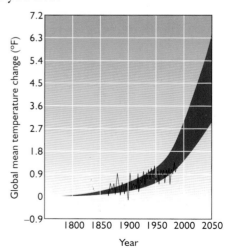

▲ ③ This graph shows how the Earth's temperature has changed over the last two centuries. The red band shows what might happen in the future.

El Niño

Every five or six years **DROUGHT** sometimes comes to regions that otherwise had plentiful rain, the monsoon fails, and elsewhere floods are far more serious than normal.

These disaster-prone years are called **EL NIÑO YEARS**, after the Spanish name for the Christ Child, since disasters begin to happen around Christmas time.

The disasters are caused by changes in the Pacific Ocean. Normally winds blow hot Pacific waters from east to west (from Peru to Indonesia). The peoples of the West Pacific, those in northern Australia and Southeast Asia, rely on the hot surface water as the source of moisture for their monsoon.

In an El Niño year the winds die down, so the water slowly spreads back eastwards (picture ④). In the West Pacific the ocean becomes cooler, less moisture evaporates, and the monsoons release less rain – they 'fail'. At the same time, the desert lands of North and South America experience a monsoon and become drenched in torrential rainfall.

These changes in the Pacific are so large that they push many of the world's weather systems out of position, leading to a whole chain of worldwide disasters (pictures ⑤ and ⑥).

▼ ④ This red area shows the places where the Pacific ocean changes. It is a long band off the coast of Peru. A huge amount of water is involved, covering an area of surface water the size of Europe.

▼ ⑤ This map shows the places in the world most affected by El Niño. Notice how Eastern Australia and Southeast Asia suffer drought (red), as do India and Southeast Africa, while Northeast Africa, Peru and California suffer torrential rainstorms (green).

▼ ⑥ Disastrous fires are an important El Niño effect. In recent years widespread fires have raged in El Niño drought areas, for example Australia and Indonesia.

Glossary

ACID RAIN Rain that has been polluted with acid gases.

AIR PRESSURE The weight of the atmosphere caused by gravity pulling gas molecules towards the centre of the Earth. A region of high pressure is formed where air currents cause dense air to sink over a region of the Earth; in a region of low pressure air rises, and is less dense.

ALTOSTRATUS CLOUD Used to describe medium height layer clouds.

ANEMOMETER An instrument for measuring wind speed.

ANTICYCLONE A high pressure area in the lower atmosphere. An anticyclone contains sinking air, and cloud is uncommon.

BAROMETER An instrument for measuring the pressure of the atmosphere.

BEAUFORT SCALE A scale for measuring wind speed in units from force 0 (calm) to force 12 (hurricane force).

BLIZZARD A snowstorm accompanied by driving winds such that the snow moves almost horizontally.

BREEZE A gentle wind. On the Beaufort scale a breeze is regarded as a flow of air less than 27 knots. *See* SEA BREEZE.

CIRRUS CLOUD Thin veil-like or wisp-like ice clouds that form in parts of the atmosphere where only ice crystals (snowflakes) can form.

CITY WEATHER The warmer conditions that exist inside a city.

CLIMATE The long-term, or average kind of weather, that might be expected at any location over a year.

CLOUD A large number of water droplets and/or ice crystals suspended in the atmosphere.

COLD FRONT The boundary between warm and cold air immediately behind an area of low pressure.

CONDENSATION The process where water vapour changes to liquid water on contact with a cold surface. A common form of condensation is dew.

CONTINENTAL CLIMATE Continental climates occur in places away from the moderating effects of sea winds.

CUMULUS CLOUD Individual clouds that form in a sky when warmed air rises. They are especially dramatic in the Tropics and in the centres of mid-latitude continents during the hot summer season when they can bring downpours and create tornadoes.

DEPRESSION (Also called low pressure), a huge swirling mass of air in mid- and high-latitude regions of the Earth. A depression brings together cold moist air from polar regions and warm moist air from the Tropics. *See* LOW PRESSURE.

DESERT Regions of very low rainfall and extremely sparse vegetation. They cover about a sixth of the Earth's land surface. They fall into three groups: (i) hot deserts, (ii) cold deserts and (iii) rainshadow deserts.

DEW Moisture that settles on grass and other surfaces when air cools. The temperature at which dew forms is called the dew point.

DRIZZLE Light rain.

DROUGHT A long, unusual period without significant rainfall. Some parts of the world, particularly between latitudes 1 and 20 degrees, have a more variable rainfall pattern than others and so they can be said to be more drought-prone.

EL NIÑO A global change in the world's weather that occurs about every five or six years.

EVAPORATION The loss of water from a surface due to the drying effect of the air.

EYE The central calm region of a tropical cyclone.

FOG Cloud that forms at ground level. Cold sea or land conditions cause the air to cool and some of the moisture in it condenses into tiny water droplets. The more water droplets that form, the thicker the fog. The thinnest form of fog is called mist.

FRONT Used by meteorologists to describe the boundary between two types of air in the atmosphere. Fronts are nearly always marked by a broad belt of cloud and rain.

FROST Occurs when moisture in the air freezes onto surfaces, producing a thin film of ice crystals. Freezing normally occurs when the temperature of the surface falls below 0°C.

GALE A strong wind: Force 8 (gale), force 9 (severe gale), force 10 (full gale or storm) on the Beaufort scale.

GLOBAL WARMING The gradual warming of the atmosphere due to the Greenhouse Effect.

GREENHOUSE EFFECT The gradual warming of the world's atmosphere due to the increase in the amount of carbon dioxide in the air.

HAIL Frozen ice that has been formed as raindrops are moved up and down through a tall cumulus cloud.

HAZE Reduced visibility caused by the build-up of dust particles in the air.

HEAT The part of the Sun's energy that causes temperature to rise.

HEAT ISLAND The region around a city which remains up to several degrees warmer than the surrounding countryside, either on still summer nights or during calm spells in winter.

HIGH PRESSURE The build-up of air in a part of the atmosphere. It is often used as an alternative to anticyclone.

HOAR FROST A build-up of ice crystals on a surface during frosty weather.

HUMIDITY The relative moisture content of the air; more properly relative humidity.

HURRICANE *See* TROPICAL CYCLONE.

ISOBAR A line drawn on a chart to represent places having the same atmospheric pressure. Isobars help to predict the strength of the wind because the closer the isobars lie, the stronger the wind will be.

LEEWARD The side sheltered from the wind.

LIGHTNING A natural spark between different layers of a cloud or between a cloud and the ground.

LOCAL WEATHER The particular regional effects that show up when the air is calm.

LOW PRESSURE A part of the atmosphere where air rises causing changeable weather. Another word used is depression.

MARITIME CLIMATE A climate that is influenced by closeness to a large body of water, usually an ocean, that experiences onshore winds.

MAXIMUM The highest value.

MID-LATITUDES The band of Earth between the Tropics and the Arctic or Antarctic.

MINIMUM The lowest value.

MIST *See* FOG.

MOISTURE *See* HUMIDITY.

MONSOON A rainy season which starts very abruptly. Countries that experience monsoons are all within, or close to the Tropics. The monsoon is particularly associated with India.

NIMBUS A name for rain-bearing clouds: cumulonimbus is used for tall thunderclouds; nimbostratus for thick rain-bearing layer clouds.

OVERCAST SKY A sky that is covered with clouds, usually layer clouds.

PRECIPITATION A general term for all forms of water particles – rain, snow, sleet, dew, hail, etc.

PREVAILING WIND The most commonly occurring wind direction.

RAINFALL Droplets of moisture that have become big enough to fall out of clouds. They are one form of precipitation.

RAINGAUGE An instrument for measuring rainfall.

RAINSHADOW Used to describe areas lying in the lee of mountain barriers that receive less rainfall than areas on the windward side of the barrier.

SEA BREEZE A coastal wind set up by the heating effect of the land relative to the sea.

SEASONS Periods of the year which have a marked character (e.g. summer is hot; a dry season has very little rain).

SMOG A combination of fog and smoke.

SNOWFLAKES Snow is made of small crystals of frozen water – ice crystals – high up in cold clouds. A snowflake is a group of ice crystals that have become heavy enough to fall from a cloud.

STORM The name for severe weather with heavy rain and strong winds. The most severe forms of storms are tropical cyclones, also called hurricanes, and typhoons.

STORM SURGE A very high tide driven onshore by a tropical cyclone.

STRATUS CLOUD The word stratus means layer. Stratus clouds are layer clouds, usually in the mid and high altitudes. Stratus cloud at ground level is experienced as fog.

SUNSHINE For weather, this is the heat energy from the Sun.

THERMAL An upward-moving flow of warm air caused by ground heating. Cumulus clouds form as a result of thermals.

THERMOMETER An instrument for measuring temperature.

THUNDER The sound produced by a lightning flash.

THUNDERSTORM A storm that is localised to a single thundercloud. Thunder is associated with tall cumulonimbus clouds.

TORNADO Originally the Spanish word for thunderstorm, tornadoes are violently spinning funnels of air that follow the base of severe thunderstorm clouds.

TROPICAL CYCLONE A name for severe low pressure regions that develop in and near to the tropics.

TROPICS The region between the Tropics of Cancer and Capricorn.

TWISTER A common name for a tornado.

TYPHOON *See* TROPICAL CYCLONE.

WARM FRONT A sloping boundary between cold and warm air in a depression. A place where cloud and rain are most likely.

WATER CYCLE The way that moisture circulates as vapour, liquid and solid between land and air.

WATERSPOUT A tornado over water.

WEATHER The short-term nature of the atmosphere. People ask "What will the weather be like tomorrow?"

WEATHER FRONT The region where cool air meets warm air. A place of cloud and rain. *See* COLD FRONT *and* WARM FRONT.

WET AND DRY SEASONS The seasons that people experience in much of the Tropics.

WHIRLWIND A violently spiralling column of air, similar to, but smaller than, a tornado. Whirlwinds have many regional names including 'dust devil' and 'willy willy'.

WIND The rapid movement of air.

WIND SOCK A conical instrument used to measure wind speed and direction.

WIND VANE A plate that swivels in a wind to show wind direction.

Index